THIS IS ME
Getting to know yourself and others better

Written by Helena Haraštová
Illustrated by Ana Kobern

I would like to thank
the psychologist Mgr. Lucie Miškóci.
Without her kind and meticulous professional
advice this book would not have been possible.

 albatros

Table of contents

EVERYBODY'S DIFFERENT!

What are you like?

We can say a lot about who we are, but it can be tough to find just the right words. Still, it helps to know and name different ways people can be, so we can talk about our needs and feelings, and understand our friends and family.

You are one of a kind

Everyone has their own special traits and talents. You can see how different people are, even little kids.

Good or bad characteristics?

No personality trait is good or bad on its own. Each one can be helpful or sometimes cause someone to act in the wrong way. This is completely normal.

We all change

We all go through different things in life, and these things shape us. They can change, strengthen, or weaken who we are and what we can do. Our feelings can come quickly, and we can't always control them right away. But we can learn to control how we act by controlling our behavior.

Getting to know each other

In this book, we'll look at different traits and abilities that people have. Our guides will be kids just like you.

They each have their own personalities and are learning how to live with them. They feel happy sometimes and sad sometimes, just like we all do.

But before we get started, let's answer some basic questions . . .

WHAT IS A **CHARACTERISTIC**?
A characteristic is a part of our personality that shows what we're like inside, how we usually act, how we react to others, and how we express ourselves. Some examples of characteristics are being sensitive, determined, or trusting.

WHAT IS AN **ABILITY**?
An ability is something you get better at through practice, experience, and learning. People have all sorts of abilities, like focusing, understanding others' feelings, and solving problems.

WHAT IS AN **EMOTION**?
An emotion is a strong feeling that affects how we act. It shows how we feel about different situations and how we respond to them. Some of the main emotions we feel are fear, anger, love, and joy.

This is Olivia.

Sometimes Olivia is **HASTY**.

Sometimes Olivia is **BRAVE**.

Max was so hastily eager to go out for a walk that Olivia didn't even have time to open the gate.

Tony wanted to cut his hair himself, but now he realizes it was a hasty decision.

Firefighters have to be brave to tackle blazing fires.

Even though Mom is afraid of heights, she bravely climbed the tree to rescue little Daisy.

What is hastiness?

Every now and then, Olivia acts or says something hastily. For example, one day, when visiting her cousin Agatha, she said, "You think up the silliest games!" After that, Agatha didn't want to play with her anymore.

Olivia was upset because she didn't like the rules of Agatha's game, and the hurtful words just slipped out. But don't worry – this is just how our brains work. Stopping and thinking is something we all must learn over time. It's not always easy . . .

HOW DO YOU KNOW YOU'RE ACTING HASTILY?

→ You do the first thing that comes into your head without thinking about it.

→ You don't think about whether your actions might be dangerous.

→ If you stopped and thought about it, you'd find a better solution.

One day, just before her birthday party, Olivia opened the fridge. The cake inside was simply too irresistible!

By the time she realized her mistake, it was too late.

Acting hastily means not thinking about what might happen next. And because our first ideas aren't always the wisest, we might later regret our actions.

But don't worry – everyone is hasty sometimes. Ask an adult about the last time they acted hastily. And what about you? When was the last time you acted hastily?

The opposite of being hasty is being careful. When Federico's sister's ball rolled into the road, he made sure they waited carefully for all the cars to pass by before retrieving it

What is bravery?

It's important to know, though, that a quick decision isn't always a hasty one. Brave people can also decide fast, even when they're scared. Their quick, careful thinking helps them make smart choices.

When Alice had to show her school project to the class, she felt nervous. But she gathered all her courage and stood up in front of everyone. To her surprise, all her classmates were very interested in what she had to say.

It takes a lot of courage to rescue someone.

Firefighters and police officers are trained to stay calm in dangerous situations. This is true in our everyday lives too. The more you conquer your fears, the easier it becomes to be brave again.

Courage isn't just about doing big, heroic things, though. It's also brave to go into the dark cellar to get Grandma's homemade jam! Whenever you face your fears, that's when you're showing how brave you are.

With a little bravery and a loyal friend beside you, you can explore the darkness of night to search for a lost toy.

This is Diego.

Sometimes Diego is
OVERSENSITIVE.

Sometimes
Diego is
PERCEPTIVE.

Isabella gets very touchy if someone doesn't like her clothes.

Phillip is inconsolable. He's taking his defeat particularly badly today.

Ada's new teacher is perceptive. She understands that everyone is nervous when they start a new class.

Frankie has decided that hot tea will make his mother feel better. He's very perceptive.

What is oversensitivity?

Every day, Diego gets bothered by many different things: like when a stranger frowns at him on the bus, when his friends argue, when he reads a sad story, or when he hears a silly joke. What upsets Diego most is that while he feels overwhelmed, his friends seem perfectly fine.

Here's another movie making Diego cry. Why isn't anyone else in the theater crying?

There's no need for Diego to worry, though. He just feels things a bit more deeply than others. We're all born with different levels of sensitivity – and any level is totally fine.

Sometimes a hug is all that's needed, sometimes kind words. And sometimes just a smile and an offer to help is enough.

Even so, Diego sometimes wishes he wasn't so sensitive. Being very sensitive – which we call *oversensitivity* – can sometimes make him feel helpless and sad. And if you're sensitive like Diego, you can learn to handle your sensitivity. It's not easy, but once you do, you'll see that it helps you notice the world's finer details.

WHAT TO DO IF YOU ARE FEELING TOO SENSITIVE:

→ Remember that whatever you are feeling now will soon pass.

→ Keep in mind that your friends maybe don't mean to hurt your feelings. Try to explain to them why you feel hurt.

In childhood, dealing calmly with sadness and disappointment can be especially hard. Sometimes, even a small thing, like a balloon popping, can feel overwhelming.

What is perceptiveness?

Sensitive people are often very perceptive. Sensing how others feel is a wonderful gift. It allows us to treat others the way we'd want to be treated.

If your friend were to bump his knee against something hard, you'd definitely notice his pain. But he might also be feeling a lot of emotions: shame because others saw the accident, disappointment because he wanted to do a new trick on his scooter like his brother, and maybe even anger because a big rock was in the way. Understanding this can help you support your friend better.

Being perceptive can be challenging, but we all learn to become more perceptive throughout our lives.

It's wonderful to have someone close who helps us when we have trouble dealing with our feelings.

Even if you don't succeed at something, try not to be sad – it's your hard work that matters.

This is Fatimah.

Sometimes
Fatimah is
UNRULY.

Sometimes
Fatimah is
ENERGETIC.

Today Elijah is pushing things too far. Why is he being so unruly?

Sam and Marie are really out of control! Let's hope they don't break something.

Kids always have fun outside. They're so full of energy.

Grandpa is still full of energy too. He just loves baking cakes for the grandkids.

What is unruliness?

Fatimah has so much energy that sitting quietly at a table is just too boring for her. Fatimah loves to run, jump, and play freely, happily making noise along the way. When she's outside at the playground being loud, she's not bothering anyone – because it's usually okay to be loud outdoors.

Fatimah caused a commotion at the doctor's during her check-up, leaving her dad flustered.

But sometimes Fatimah releases her energy in the wrong place or at the wrong time. If she doesn't rein herself in, she becomes uncontrollable: ignoring instructions, refusing to listen, and unaware that her behavior is disruptive.

It's really fun to burn off energy at the playground!

It's easy to let yourself go, especially when you're having fun or trying to be less bored. The problem is, what we find funny might bother others.

What is being energetic?

For someone with a lot of energy, it's really hard to sit still and do nothing. The trick is to do something fun that doesn't bother anyone. What can you put that energy into? Baking

Some adults like to burn off excess energy by getting exercise.

cakes, solving puzzles, hiking in the countryside, or building blocks – whatever sounds fun to you!

If you feel you're about to lose self-control, pause for a moment and look around: How do others see your behavior? Is it bothering them? Could you hurt someone? If so, try sitting down and taking a deep breath. Having lots of energy can actually help us improve the world around us. How about organizing a litter clean-up or brightening your classroom with colorful drawings? Or maybe painting a hopscotch court in the park for other kids to play on?

Some people go hiking in the countryside to burn off their energy.

This is Tina.

Sometimes Tina is
SHY.

Sometimes
Tina is
THOUGHTFUL.

Anette shyly hides behind her mother. She is wary of people she doesn't know.

Joel would like to get involved in his classmates' conversation, but he's too shy.

May is a thoughtful little girl and a great listener.

Our scout leader is a quiet person, but he writes articles about his travels. You should read them – they're amazing!

What is shyness?

Tina feels anxious even in ordinary situations like meeting new people, handling unexpected tasks, or speaking in front of others. She's very shy, and many others feel the same way. Shy people are the unsung heroes of everyday life, because they face challenging situations and manage to deal with them.

Sometimes it helps if we rehearse a stressful situation in advance.

Some of us are naturally inclined to shyness, and unpleasant experiences can sometimes worsen it. But just remember – there's nothing wrong with being alone sometimes, if that makes you comfortable.

Tina felt too shy to wear a costume to the parade, but she still wanted to participate. So she and her mother joined without costumes, and she ended up having a fantastic time.

HOW DO YOU OVERCOME SHYNESS?

→ Whatever stressful situation you're facing, rehearse it at home beforehand.

→ Don't hesitate to ask your parents, a teacher, or a friend for help.

→ Gain experience – the more you face similar situations, the quicker your shyness will fade.

→ If you want to join a group outing, a school party, or a dance lesson, imagine yourself already participating and enjoying it.

→ If you decide you'd rather not participate in an event, don't blame yourself. Just allow yourself the comfort of some peace and solitude.

What is thoughtfulness?

Sometimes Tina's shyness isn't a problem at all. It gives her a chance to ponder her interests and come up with fantastic ideas. Many people are comfortable being quiet and reserved. They find peace spending time alone with their thoughts.

Over time, though, shy people can learn to handle tough situations without feeling uncomfortable. As they grow up, they become more confident and decide when they want to be with friends and talk, or when they'd prefer to be alone and quiet.

Shy Tina has always loved art, even as a girl. When she grew up, she became a gallery curator. Now, she gets to study art quietly by herself, but she also talks confidently to excited visitors at art shows.

21

This is Elias.

Sometimes Elias is
TALKATIVE.

Sometimes
Elias is
COMMUNICATIVE.

Two chatty ladies were babbling next to us at the movies. They were disturbing everyone around them.

Felix's chatty parrot Peanut talks from morning to night – that bird just won't shut up!

Felix is very interested in animals and is very communicative. He quickly made friends with the zookeeper.

Malik is a communicative boy, so he quickly found friends at the beach.

What is talkativeness?

Elias is a friendly boy, but he sometimes doesn't know when to stop talking. His head is full of interesting ideas, and he's always eager to share them with others.

Talkative people are usually very friendly, kind, and warm-hearted. The problem is, they sometimes don't know when to stop. Other people need moments of silence to think or share their own opinions.

Sometimes it's okay to talk, and other times it's best to be quiet.

When you constantly feel the need to talk, sing, or make noises, try using an anti-stress ball, which you can easily make yourself from an inflatable balloon and flour.

Elias's story started out nice, and it was pretty funny, but it went on and on . . .

In the end, Elias's talkativeness was too much, even for himself, and he fell asleep just before they arrived.

HOW DO YOU KNOW YOU'RE BEING OVERTALKATIVE?

→ You've been talking about many things, one after another, not letting anyone get a word in.

→ Those listening are interested at first, but soon they lose interest.

→ You feel like you have to talk just to avoid silence.

For example, if your friends are tired or busy, they might not have the energy to listen to your thoughts. If you pay attention to others and notice when they want to listen and when they don't, people will be more eager to hear you. Can you remember a time when someone talked so much that it started to bother you?

Kendrick starts telling the teacher what he did over the weekend – in the middle of a math lesson.

What is being communicative?

When you keep talking without stopping, others can get irritated or angry. Try to wait for the right time to talk. Your friends will be happy to hear what you think of the play or the latest chapter in the textbook during the break, and you'll get to hear their thoughts too.

If you enjoy talking with others and can listen, as well as speak, you'll learn new things and how to have good conversations.

Your ability to talk easily can also help others, especially those who are too shy to start a conversation on their own. Speaking first is a special skill. If you approach someone and find they're interested in talking, you can have a fun and friendly chat. And who knows – you might even become friends.

Frankie was very happy to talk to his neighbor and ask if he needed help crossing the road safely.

This is Aaron.

Sometimes Aaron is
ARGUMENTATIVE.

Sometimes Aaron
ENJOYS DISCUSSIONS.

Lisa and Adele had an argument over choosing a ribbon for Grandma's present. Now they're not talking to each other.

Politicians often argue just like little children. Yesterday, they were doing so in front of the TV cameras!

Mr. and Mrs. Harari haven't been able to agree on what their new house should look like, but they keep discussing it.

Elijah and his grandfather are having an enjoyable discussion about vintage cars while they load the wood.

What is being argumentative?

Aaron knows that arguments can be useful sometimes. But when he's in a bad mood, it seems like he's looking for a fight. Instead of politely saying what is bothering him, he starts arguing.

When Nicole's mother asked her to help dry the dishes, Nicole responded rudely. Oh dear, it looks like an argument is coming.

ARGUMENT

→ We don't accept
the other person's opinion.
→ We insult and criticize each other.
→ We both want to get our own way.
→ We both end up losing.

Rex and Rocky fought so much over the toy that they destroyed it. Now they both have nothing to play with.

WE SHOULD . . .

→ Listen to and respect other people's opinions.
→ Talk to each other politely.
→ Look for a solution that suits both of us.

Rex and Rocky decided to play tug-of-war with the toy. What a grrrrrrreat game!

Aaron is getting angry. He thinks his friend has not shared the candy fairly.

When we're in an argumentative mood, we fight over silly little things. Later, we might regret it because, in our anger, we sometimes say hurtful things to the people we love.

If you want to keep good relationships with others, treating them politely and respectfully.

What does it mean to enjoy discussions?

During an argument, each person tries to win. In a discussion, though, both sides look for things they can agree on. Exchanging opinions, ideas, and experiences helps us better understand the world.

Friendly discussions can help us understand each other better. Even when we disagree, we can stay friends. For example, if you love sunlight but your friend hates the heat, you might both enjoy swimming and have a great time together at the pool.

Instead of getting into unnecessary conflicts, you can deepen your friendships through meaningful discussions about different topics.

Aaron and his friend are figuring out how to make things from paper. When one of them can't think of anything, the other comes up with an idea.

This is Clara.

Sometimes Clara is
PERSEVERING.

30

Ethan stubbornly refuses to eat his vegetables. He only wants sweet things . . .

Uncle George insisted on not taking the bus to the airport. So he loaded his luggage onto his scooter. As a result, he lost one of his suitcases.

Neither the challenging terrain nor the heavy backpack could stop Aunt Paula. With great perseverance, she climbed to the top.

Emily knows you need to persevere in order to house-train a dog. That's why she takes her puppy outside, even at night.

What is stubbornness?

Ever since she was a toddler, Clara has insisted that her way is the right way. Clara is incredibly creative in inventing new ways of doing things.

It is evening and Clara stubbornly refuses to prepare her bag for school tomorrow.

However, sometimes Clara's ways can bother others – and even herself. For instance, not long ago, she wanted to wear a fairy costume on a class field trip. Another time, she insisted on having chocolate cake for dinner. Just imagine what might have happened if she had succeeded!

"I'm not holding your hand, Dad!" insists Jayden.

"Help, Dad! I'm falling!" Jayden's stubbornness backfires.

HOW DO YOU KNOW YOU'RE BEING STUBBORN?

→ You don't want to listen to other people's advice, even when you think they're reasonable.

→ You refuse to change your attitude, opinion, or approach, even if it's not working.

→ Sometimes you do something you've been told not to do.

Doing things your own way can be great, as long as it's not unsafe or disrespectful to others. Like when you're supposed to be getting dressed to go visit someone and your entire family and everyone is waiting for you to hurry up, it's important to get ready on time.

What is perseverance?

The flip-side of being stubborn is having a strong determination to pursue your goals and persisting until you achieve them. We call this perseverance, and it can really help us succeed in life. A persevering person keeps trying until they reach their goals. Unlike stubbornness, though, perseverance doesn't cause trouble or bother anyone else.

Clara can be very persevering. When she decided to make a fairy dress, she learned how to sew. She was rightly proud of what she had achieved.

If you're sometimes stubborn, it means you have a strong will. If you use it wisely, you can achieve a lot in life!

Even though Japanese is a challenging language, Helena is passionate about it. Thanks to her perseverance, she can already communicate in everyday situations.

A year ago, it seemed as if Cade would never become a dancer. Now look at him!

This is Destiny.

Sometimes
Destiny
DAYDREAMS.

Sometimes
Destiny is
FOCUSED.

34

Edith was daydreaming while walking her dog in the park, and she nearly stepped on Fifi's tail.

Mrs. Curtis was daydreaming during the bus ride, so she forgot to get off at the right stop.

When Georgina is fully focused on her painting, she can create beautiful works due to her vivid imagination.

The twins were so focused on their shadow theater! They didn't even notice it was nighttime already.

What is daydreaming?

Destiny sometimes hears people say, "Destiny's a bit of a daydreamer" – and sometimes she doesn't hear it . . . because she's not paying attention! Often, once she starts thinking about something, she gets so lost in her thoughts that she doesn't notice what's going on around her.

Destiny daydreams about many things – if only she could make them come true!

Daydreaming can be helpful. It can get us ready for things that might happen, like performing in front

35

What better way to explore your imaginative ideas than to share them with your friends!

of others or running a race. Thinking about happy things can even make us feel calm.

But real life offers so much more. Even though Destiny is very imaginative, she also likes to play tennis with her friends, explore the forest, read books, and play the piano.

It's nice when someone wakes us up from their daydreaming. Dreams are fun but reality is even better.

What is being focused?

Sometimes, Destiny's dad forgets about the world around him too. When he's in his workshop, he gets so focused that he doesn't even notice he's hungry. But he's not daydreaming; he's making his ideas real, like creating a new toy for Destiny.

His wonderful imagination helps him create many amazing things. He's truly happy doing what he loves, in a state of intense concentration called "flow" – because it's like riding a wave of fun.

"Let's see, if I put these pieces here together, it would make a pretty cool robot for Destiny."

With a rich imagination, playing detective can be thrilling.

This is Richard.

Sometimes Richard is BOSSY.

Sometimes Richard is a LEADER.

Jake is acting like he's the boss – he wants to have the bench all to himself.

"Laura, I want to draw it my own way. Stop telling me what colors to use!"

Christine is so talented her friends love it when she leads them in a song.

Antonio works in an auto shop. Since he's the most experienced one there, he passes on his knowledge to the others.

Because Richard wouldn't listen to anyone else's ideas, his friends started playing without him.

What is bossiness?

When Richard plays with other kids, he has tons of great game ideas and likes to take charge. Sometimes, though, it can be a bit overwhelming.

At first, young children try to boss their parents around, before they learn that they only get their way by being nice.

HOW DO YOU KNOW YOU'RE BEING BOSSY?

→ You make up rules and tell others what to do.

→ You don't explain your ideas or talk things over with others.

→ You don't let others share their own ideas.

→ People often leave your games or stop listening to you pretty quickly.

Richard has a knack for leading others, which is a great gift! It's not easy, though, as he's learning. He wants to be a great leader, but sometimes he seems too . . . well, bossy.

Someone who acts bossy towards us often wants to be friends but may not know how to show it. Their bossiness might come from feeling unsure of themselves. What advice would you give them?

Since Richard is both courageous and kind, he was a natural leader on the field trip.

A proper leader never forgets that everyone can be involved in decision-making.

What is a leader?

If you want to lead others, you need to be more than just determined. A good leader also needs to have natural authority – which is when people listen closely to you because they trust your confidence.

If you have natural authority, that's great! And if you want to become a leader, you'll need to make an effort and gain experience.

You may find others naturally starting to follow you. If so, congratulate yourself! It shows you're becoming a kind and responsible leader. Leadership is a skill you can improve over time – more experience means it will come more naturally to you.

Richard dreams of becoming a movie director someday. Directing a team of actors and artists to create a blockbuster film requires focus, courage, and patience with others.

Jenny is a responsible Scout leader. She carefully records the requests and ideas of the kids in her troop to look at later when she has more time.

This is Daniel.

Sometimes Daniel is STINGY.

Sometimes Daniel is CAREFUL WITH HIS THINGS.

Our neighbor is being pretty greedy. He won't let anyone borrow his scooter, even though his leg has been in a cast for two weeks!

Francesca is being rather stingy – she won't let her sister have even the smallest taste!

Grandpa was happy to show me his album of rare stamps yesterday, but he didn't let me touch them because he was worried I might accidentally damage them.

Mom decided that the beautiful old vase that her great-grandmother left her would be displayed on the top shelf, so that no one could accidentally break it.

When Alex broke Daniel's skateboard, Daniel was not only unhappy but angry – and rightly so.

What is stinginess?

Daniel knows it's good to share, but he's had some bad experiences: toys have come back broken, a book got lost, and his candy disappeared after his friends had some. But he knows that friendship and not sharing don't mix.

Why are you kids fighting over that one block? There are plenty to go around!

Anette is playing with the teddy bear right now. Suzanne wants to borrow it, but she needs to wait a little while.

There are times when we don't feel like sharing our things. If you're playing with your toy, you don't have to give it to a friend. But you could offer them another toy so you can play together.

Young kids sometimes don't want to share. They might not know that lending a toy means they'll get it back. Over time, though, we learn it's good to share and borrow – it helps everyone have fun!

Playing with a new ball with a friend is so much fun!

What is being careful?

It's normal to worry about your things and to want to keep them safe. For example, would you let your clumsy three-year-old cousin play with the model ship on your shelf? Probably not. But what if a friend your age wanted to see it while you were there? Probably yes. And obviously you let *yourself* handle it.

The girls were delighted when Grandma carefully took her puppets out of the old chest and let them look at them.

If you worry about your favorite things, you can still enjoy them around other kids. For example, you could fly your kite while a friend helps you. Or you could look at your animal encyclopedia with a friend, carefully turning the pages yourself. It's okay to protect your things or to just want to use them yourself.

Try explaining why you don't want to lend someone something, and you can still find a way to have fun together.

Kendrick had always wanted his own drone. When he finally got one, he was very careful with it. He didn't let anyone else use the controls, but he invited his friends to come watch it fly.

So what are any of us really like?

Everyone is different, with their own mix of good and bad traits, moods, and days when they're not at their best. Our actions are influenced by how we feel, what we've been through, and our natural tendencies. Sometimes we show our not-so-good side, and other times we show our best – that's totally normal!

When we see that we've done something wrong, it takes courage to say we're sorry. This means overcoming fear or shame. Saying "I'm sorry" can make a big difference! Take a look around and think about why people act the way they do.

What do they want and need? As we "people watch" everyone in this park – and throughout our journey in life – let's get to know each other better. Great idea, don't you think?

THIS IS ME

Getting to know yourself and others better

© B4U Publishing for Albatros,
an imprint of Albatros Media Group, 2025
5. května 1746/22, Prague 4, Czech Republic

Author: Helena Haraštová
Illustrator: © Ana Kobern, 2024
Editors: Helena Haraštová, Radka Píro
Translator: Mark Worthington
Proofreader: Scott Alexander Jones
Expert consultant: Lucie Miškóci
Graphics and typesetting: Martin Urbánek

Printed in China by Leo Paper Group Ltd.

www.albatrosbooks.com

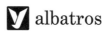